THIS WALKER BOOK BELONGS TO:

_____

_____

_____

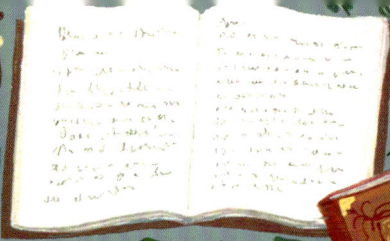
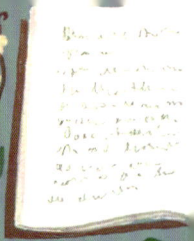

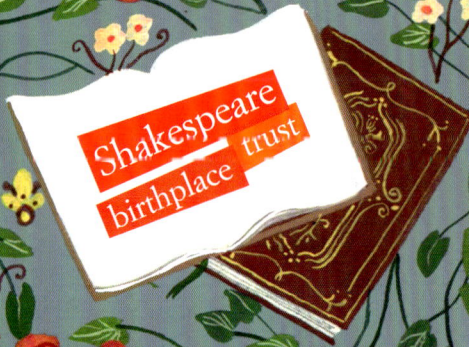

Shakespeare birthplace trust

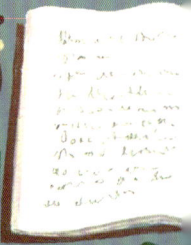

Bold and Brave Women

from SHAKESPEARE

ILLUSTRATED BY

Becca Stadtlander

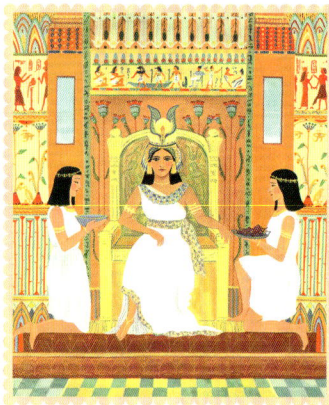

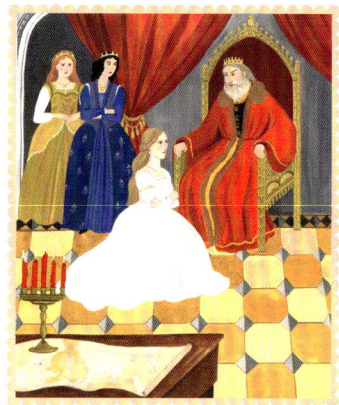

Meet this cast of bold and brave women from Shakespeare.

Twelve of Shakespeare's heroines are richly and gorgeously given life in this collection. From Juliet leaning out of her window to the battle-ready Margaret of Anjou, this book celebrates the diversity of Shakespeare's women on their own terms.

Portia, known for being rich and beautiful, rightly appears here in her male disguise as the lawyer Balthazar. The ambitious Lady Macbeth is no sleepwalking subject of pity, but a determined woman looking out towards her promised future.

All of these women are individuals. Funny, flawed, naïve, selfish and even sometimes plain rude, these characters are wonderfully nuanced portraits of human beings. Juliet refuses to be compliant and defies her parents; the sprightly Rosalind oozes joy out of the very pores of her being. Even the dynamic duo of Mistress Ford and

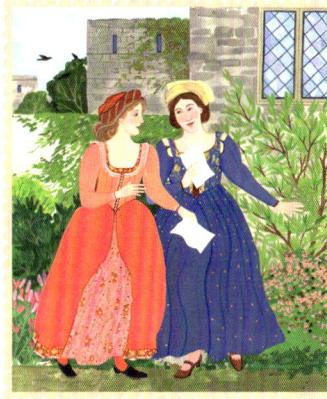

Mistress Page, united in their rejection of sleazy Falstaff, have distinct personalities. Cordelia, for all her loyalty to her father, is frustrating in her stubbornness, and the regal Cleopatra is egocentric beyond measure.

We might not champion their choices and actions, but it is still possible to celebrate the initiative of Portia, the resourcefulness of Rosalind, the loyalty of Beatrice, the majesty of Cleopatra and the sheer force of Margaret of Anjou.

For audiences young and old, this is a wonderful introduction to the magic of Shakespeare's stories and the richness of his characters. What more charming way is there to enjoy Shakespeare than with this beautifully illustrated introduction to the women in his best-known plays? Both bold and brave indeed.

Anjna Chouhan

Senior Lecturer in Shakespeare Studies, Shakespeare Birthplace Trust

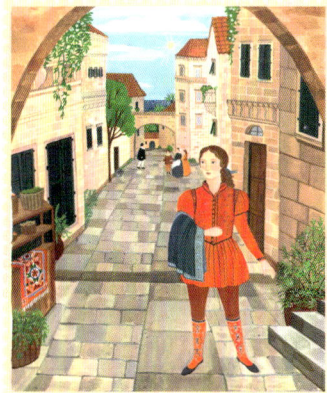

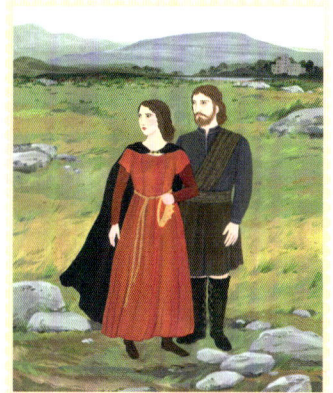

Titania

A Midsummer Night's Dream

And for her sake do I rear up her boy;
And for her sake I will not part with him
(ACT 2, SCENE 1)

Jealous Oberon commands that I give him my beloved changeling boy;
for he is King of the Fairies and King of me. But I am Queen of the Fairies;
*the forest does **my** bidding, Nature tells **my** woes. So I raise my head in*
the moonlight and reply: "Not for thy fairy kingdom!"

Titania, Queen of the Fairies, is quarrelling with Oberon, her husband and King of the Fairies. Oberon demands that his wife give him the human boy she has adopted, but Titania flatly refuses. The boy's mother was a loyal servant of Titania's and she vowed to care for the child when his mother died. The boy has become her joy and Oberon wishes to take that from her.

But Titania knows her own mind: she shuns living with Oberon during their quarrel and is not afraid to accuse her husband of having relationships with other women. As Queen of the Fairies, Titania commands powerful magic, and her dispute with Oberon becomes so violent that even Nature's order is disrupted. Storms rage and the crops will not grow, but still Titania refuses to give up the boy.

Because Titania will not bow to his will, Oberon resorts to trickery. He commands his sprite Puck to enchant her with a love potion while she is sleeping in her bower; when she awakes, Titania will fall in love with the first creature she sets eyes upon. This creature is Bottom, a weaver to whom Puck has given the head of an ass. Under the spell, Titania fawns over Bottom, making her the fool of the forest. When Oberon lifts the enchantment, she is confused to recall a strange dream in which she was in love with an ass. The haughty Queen of the Fairies obeys Oberon at last, but only because of an enchantment and not because the fight was fairly won.

Cleopatra

Antony and Cleopatra

> *I am fire and air*
> (ACT 5, SCENE 2)

I was Queen of all Egypt. I ruled my lands, a woman alone. I commanded men at war and ships at sea. I stole Rome's greatest general from them, and I commanded him, too. They said I was a temptress, a danger to the mighty Republic of Rome. They were right.

Cleopatra, Queen of Egypt, is renowned for her power and beauty. She is passionately in love with the great Roman general, Antony, but their relationship is uneasy. The Romans and Egyptians are troubled allies, so despite the strength of their feelings, the lovers cannot fully trust each other.

Cleopatra knows she can fascinate the men who wish to control her, and she ruthlessly protects her independence. She can be jealous and unpredictable, playing games with those who are captivated by her. When Antony falls under her spell, he is mocked by his fellow Romans for neglecting his duty as a soldier and turning his back on Roman values.

The lovers fall out, mistrusting each other's intentions and loyalty. Finally they pledge to fight together against Octavius, Antony's rival in Rome, but Cleopatra abandons Antony in the middle of the battle at sea. He follows her back to Egypt, dishonouring himself as a soldier by deserting his troops. Antony blames Cleopatra for his behaviour and threatens to kill her over her betrayal. To win back her lover's affection, Cleopatra fakes her own death – but Antony is so devastated by the news that he turns his sword on himself. Antony dies in her arms and Cleopatra is captured by the Romans – but, her own woman to the last, she refuses to become Rome's slave. Dressing in her royal garments, she brings a poisonous snake to her breast and chooses to join Antony in a love beyond death. Her story of passion, power and politics has become immortal.

Rosalind

As You Like It

> " *I have promised to make all this matter even*
> (ACT 5, SCENE 4) "

Call me Rosalind the maid, call me Ganymede the youth:
I am swashing in both skins. I begin and end this story a
woman, but I play it in doublet and hose, roaming free and
merry as a fellow through the Forest of Arden.

Rosalind has been raised in the court of wicked Duke Frederick, as a companion to the Duke's daughter, Celia. When the Duke turns against Rosalind, the two girls run away to the Forest of Arden in search of Rosalind's father. Inside the magical forest, normal rules do not apply and Rosalind can try on different identities.

Rosalind is a force to be reckoned with. When things turn against her, she applies her sharp mind and gutsy spirit to make the most of the situation. When she is banished from her home, she sees an opportunity for travel; when she realizes that two girls wandering the forest alone could be dangerous, she disguises herself as a boy, Ganymede, so she can protect her cousin, Celia. In the forest, Rosalind and Celia have fun together, laughing and joking, free from all the rules on how women should behave at court.

Rosalind is even able to choose her lover, Orlando. Disguised as Ganymede, she then makes a project of training him to be her equal. Using her quick wits, she tricks him into a role-playing game in which she pretends to be Rosalind, so Orlando can practise his courtship. She mocks his overblown ideas of romantic love and lovelorn verses, preferring to speak her mind. Clever, sparky and resourceful, Rosalind sees life and love as a mad game to be played with a smile and a knowing wink.

Margaret of Anjou

Henry VI Parts I–III and Richard III

> *She-wolf of France ...*
> *Whose tongue more poisons than the adder's tooth*
> (HENRY VI, PART III, ACT I, SCENE 4)

She-wolf. Tigress. More like a man than a woman.
They think to insult me with these words, but I receive them
all as virtues. I am not here to be loved. I am here to rule.

Margaret of Anjou is ferocious – she thrives in the twisted world of court politics and commands armies in the field. She is a warrior queen who cares nothing for people or justice, but only for advancing her cause. There is chain mail in her soul.

Her husband, King Henry VI, is weak, so she herself takes command of the army of Lancaster during the Wars of the Roses, in which the Houses of Lancaster and York fight for control of the throne. When the King's friend and protector, Gloucester, blocks her path to power, she retaliates by having him murdered. Margaret scorns what she sees as womanly softness, and only pretends to feel fear in order to fool her enemies into underestimating her. She sees violence as necessary for power and is strong enough to take action. When a peace treaty with the Duke of York disinherits her son from the throne, she raises an army and stabs York on the battlefield – but not before she has waved a handkerchief stained with his young son's blood before his eyes.

When her own son and heir is killed in front of her, she finally reveals a broken humanity, begging to die alongside him. But instead she is forced to live out her days in her enemy's castle, reduced to a bitter old woman who mutters curses against all the rivals who have taken her family's throne. As a woman in a man's world of political intrigue, Margaret fights with every weapon she has, unafraid of others' judgement.

Cordelia

King Lear

> *So young, my lord, and true*
> (ACT I, SCENE I)

I am the third daughter, the favourite of our father, the old King; I show him my care and duty daily, in deeds not words. My cruel sisters speak falsely to win his favours, but I cannot – will not – heave my heart into my mouth. I am Cordelia, the daughter who loves truth more than power.

Cordelia is the youngest of King Lear's three daughters, favoured for her beauty and kindness. But when the vain King sets the sisters against each other, asking them to profess how much they love him in order to win a share of his kingdom, Cordelia refuses to flatter him, telling him that she loves him according to her duty as a daughter, not more, not less. She is bravely honest and deeply loving, even when those around her are not.

Lear casts her out in a rage and divides his kingdom between her two scheming sisters, the power-hungry Goneril and Regan. Cordelia reluctantly leaves her father at their mercy and flees with her new husband, the King of France. Once they have taken Lear's throne, Goneril and Regan mistreat their father, driving him to madness.

Brave Cordelia returns to rescue her father. When she sees the pitiful state Lear has been reduced to, she tenderly cares for him and Lear finally understands that she is his only true daughter. But the revelation comes too late. Cordelia's army is defeated. Rather than fleeing to safety in France, she stays with her ruined father, resulting in her execution and Lear's death from grief. Although of a gentle disposition, Cordelia shows strength and integrity by insisting on the truth. She stubbornly refuses to compromise herself in an unjust situation; she quietly pursues what she knows in her heart to be right.

Lady Macbeth

Macbeth

> *Fill me from the crown to the toe top-full*
> *Of direst cruelty!*
> (ACT I, SCENE 5)

Murderess. Monster. Madwoman. The voices echo about the castle as I walk the night, seeking absolution where none can be found. Blood on my hands, poison in my veins, a stolen crown on my head. But what is done cannot be undone; my hands will never be clean.

Lady Macbeth is ambitious. When her husband, the honourable warrior Macbeth, tells her that three witches have prophesied that he will become King of Scotland, she becomes obsessed with power. But for Macbeth to take the throne, and for her to become Queen of Scotland, the current King, Duncan, would have to die – or be killed.

So Lady Macbeth persuades her husband to murder King Duncan, whispering treachery in his ear and goading him to act more like a man. When Macbeth wavers over her plot, she is so frustrated by his weakness that she summons murderous spirits to take away her humanity and make her less like a woman, so that she might carry out the murder herself. She drugs the King's guards, allowing Macbeth to prove himself by killing Duncan, then she smears the guards with the King's blood to make them look guilty of the crime. She is stronger, more ruthless and more manipulative than her husband, and seems unafraid of violence.

But with the first murder complete, the couple's roles reverse; Macbeth spirals into more killing in order to keep the throne and Lady Macbeth becomes consumed with guilt. She descends into madness, sleepwalking about the castle muttering of dark deeds and trying to wash invisible bloodstains from her hands. At her death she is a ruin of her former self, but the consequences of her cruelty and power-lust cannot be washed away.

Beatrice

Much Ado About Nothing

> " *My dear Lady Disdain* "
> (ACT I, SCENE I)

My Lady Tongue, they say of me; Beatrice the scold – quick to scorn, slow to love. I talk up a merry storm, words flying fast, and no man can stem the flow of my wits. My uncle would "fit me with a husband". I say, show me the man who would fit Beatrice.

Beatrice, an orphan who lives with her uncle and beloved cousin, Hero, in Sicily, is a young woman with a fearsome reputation for being sharp-tongued and strong-willed. Scornful of men and marriage, she laughs at the absurdity of life and vows to keep her independence.

She engages in a war of verbal wits with the soldier Benedick, who has hurt Beatrice in the past and has also renounced marriage. They exchange clever and funny insults as if they would talk themselves mad. In a fit of mischief, their friends plot to trick the two into falling in love through a game of overheard conversations. Despite her initial refusal to be overmastered by any man, Beatrice talks herself into loving Benedick back. But she is cautious about falling in love, not wanting to make herself vulnerable.

Beatrice's cousin, Hero, is falsely accused of being unfaithful by her lover, Claudio, who is Benedick's best friend. A vengeful Beatrice demands that Benedick prove his love for her by killing Claudio. Crisis is averted and the two couples are reunited, but Beatrice will only marry Benedick on her own terms. They quarrel their way to the altar, and Beatrice makes a reluctant, wisecracking bride, whose unstoppable mouth Benedick attempts to stop with a kiss.

Juliet

Romeo and Juliet

This same wayward girl
(ACT 4, SCENE 2)

They call me true and faithful Juliet; a girl at her window, falling
in love for the first time, blowing star-crossed kisses into the
night. It's true that I fell for Romeo – it was love at first sight.
And yet I chose my love and I followed my own will to the end.

Juliet Capulet is a young woman who is set on following her heart, even if it means going against the wishes of her father. When she first meets Romeo, she doesn't know that he is a Montague, the noble family with whom the Capulets have an ancient feud. When she discovers that his family connections mean she has no hope of marrying him, she is devastated. In Lord Capulet's orchard, as dawn breaks, they declare their love for each other and devise a plan to secretly marry.

Thirteen, and on the cusp of adulthood, Juliet shows herself to be both headstrong and resolute. Her father, Lord Capulet, is expecting her to marry Paris, the nobleman of *his* choice, but Juliet is determined against it and marries Romeo in secret. When Juliet's cousin, Tybalt, kills Romeo's close friend Mercutio in a duel, Romeo responds by killing Tybalt to avenge his friend's death. The Capulet–Montague feud intensifies, but after carefully considering what happened, Juliet remains loyal to Romeo.

Juliet's father demands that she marry Paris and she decides the only way to escape is to feign death by taking a sleeping potion and then run away from their families in Verona. Though terrified of being buried alive, she says she will wait for Romeo in the Capulet family tomb without fear or doubt. But in a cruel twist of fate the plan goes wrong, and both lovers are left dead. The grieving Capulet and Montague families vow to bury their feud along with Romeo and Juliet. Although her story doesn't end happily, Juliet challenges the idea that a daughter should be ruled by her father; she remains true to herself in love.

Portia

The Merchant of Venice

> *I have within my mind*
> *A thousand raw tricks*
> (ACT 3, SCENE 4)

Quick-witted Portia, they call me; hair like gold, tongue like quicksilver, and blessed with the brains to think my way through a man's world of laws and money. I was my father's property, ready to be traded in the Venetian marriage market. But I plied my trickster wits, and made this business my own.

Portia is intelligent, beautiful and wealthy, but bound to obey the will of her dead father. He has left a test for anyone who wishes for her hand in marriage, but Portia is already in love with Bassanio, a gentleman of Venice. She decides to get the husband she wants – without breaking her father's controlling rules.

The suitor has to choose correctly from three caskets, so Portia finds clever loopholes in her father's will and devises a way to help Bassanio select the right casket and win her hand. Portia knows marriage doesn't always mean happiness, so she then tests the loyalty of her new husband by giving him a ring. When Bassanio disappoints her by giving her ring away, she gives him a lesson in what she expects from their marriage.

Portia shows she is smarter than the men around her when Bassanio's friend, Antonio, is summoned to court by a moneylender called Shylock, who wishes to claim the pound of flesh Antonio owes him for failing to settle a debt. Portia disguises herself as the young male lawyer Balthazar and wins the court case for Antonio through a brilliant display of legal logic: Shylock must spare Antonio because the law says he may take a pound of flesh but not a single drop of Antonio's blood. By the end, Portia has twisted the rules to her advantage and chosen her own husband, preventing an injustice and outwitting the men around her in the process.

Mistress Ford and Mistress Page

The Merry Wives of Windsor

Wives may be merry, and yet honest, too
(ACT 4, SCENE 2)

Mistress Ford and Mistress Page, thick as thieves we are; neither of us born yesterday, but ever ready for mirth and mischief. Knaves think to woo us out of our riches, and foolish husbands repay us with jealousy where trust is due. These puffed-up fellows are due a schooling; and we wives are due some merriment.

Mistress Ford and Mistress Page are the wives of two wealthy merchants. When a drunken knight, Falstaff, finds himself short of money, he decides to replenish his coffers by trying to woo them. But the Wives of Windsor are far from easy prey and their spirited friendship gives them the upper hand over Falstaff.

When the two friends discover they have received identical love letters from Falstaff, they decide to teach him a lesson and have some fun at his expense. They pretend to have fallen for his unlikely charms, but really plan a series of tricks to show him up. First of all, they lure Falstaff to Mistress Ford's home, then hide him in a laundry basket when her husband returns; Falstaff soon finds himself thrown in the river with the dirty washing. Their next ploy is to dress Falstaff up as an old woman, which results in Master Ford punching him.

Finding all this hilarious, the Wives plot a final humiliation. Falstaff is dressed in a hunter's costume and left at the haunted oak tree in the forest, whereupon the local children, disguised as sprites, jump out and taunt him. Mistress Ford's jealous husband realizes his mistake and declares that he will never mistrust his clever wife again. The Wives of Windsor see the funny side of life, but they are not to be fooled with. In charge of their households, the two wily friends are unstoppable when they put their heads together.

Miranda

The Tempest

"*Infused with a fortitude from heaven*"
(ACT I, SCENE 2)

I have known no other world than this island of illusions;
I have known no other human except my father, Prospero. I look
upon everything with the new eyes of a child, my mind free to wonder.
But when I set eyes on Ferdinand, I saw a brave new world.

Miranda has lived alone on a wild and remote island with her father, Prospero the magician, since she was a baby. Having had a sheltered upbringing outside of society, where her life has been completely shaped by her father, she is innocent to both the opportunities and dangers the world away from the island offers.

A terrible storm causes a shipwreck that brings her father's old political rivals, including Prince Ferdinand of Naples, to their island. Miranda suspects that Prospero has used magic to conjure the tempest. She is compassionate and pleads for the crew's safety. But unknown to her, Prospero and his sprite, Ariel, cast an enchantment over the entire island, allowing them to control everything that happens there – and for Prospero to get revenge on the men who wronged him many years ago.

Miranda wakes from Prospero's charmed sleep and falls instantly in love with Ferdinand, the first young man she has ever seen. She is forthright in expressing her feelings to Ferdinand and proposes marriage to him. Even when her father pretends to disapprove, she stands firm in her devotion. Although her love for Ferdinand is part of her father's plan, Miranda's amazement at the richness of humanity seems true in a world of sleight-of-hand tricks. Miranda is a force for good as powerful as her father's calculated magic. Her patient, caring nature helps reconcile rivalries and restore order.

Viola

Twelfth Night

I am not what I am
(ACT 3, SCENE I)

When fate cast me ashore in an unknown land, I did not lose myself as a girl but rather found myself as a boy. With the garb of a man but the true heart of a woman, I, Viola, became Cesario: the boy-girl who captivated the court of Illyria.

Viola is shipwrecked and washed ashore on Illyria. She has lost her twin brother, Sebastian, who she believes drowned in the shipwreck. Finding herself alone in a strange land, Viola decides to dress herself as a boy – Cesario – and find work as a page to Orsino, Duke of Illyria. Viola's male disguise gives her a new identity and freedom to make her own choices, but it also causes complications.

Duke Orsino is lovesick for Countess Olivia and Viola is entrusted to carry his love letters. In her disguise of Cesario, Viola unintentionally captivates Countess Olivia and also charms the Duke. Before long everyone is in love with the wrong person: Orsino loves Olivia; Olivia loves Cesario (Viola); and Cesario (Viola) has fallen in love with Orsino. Viola's constant and devoted love contrasts to the more fickle affections of the other characters.

But Viola's twin brother, Sebastian, has not, in fact, drowned. When he unexpectedly appears at Countess Olivia's house, she mistakes him for Cesario and they are married. The Duke is furious, believing that his servant has betrayed him; but when the twins are finally reunited, everyone sees that this is a case of confused identities. Viola reveals herself as a woman and becomes engaged to Duke Orsino. She has successfully turned the court of Illyria upside down, causing those she encounters to question their understanding of what it means to be male and female.

For Maggie – L.E.

First published 2020 by Walker Books Ltd
87 Vauxhall Walk, London SE11 5HJ
in association with the
Shakespeare Birthplace Trust
Henley Street, Stratford-upon-Avon
Warwickshire CV37 6QW

This edition published 2024

2 4 6 8 10 9 7 5 3 1

Text © 2020 Walker Books Ltd
Illustrations © 2020 Rebecca Stadtlander

The right of Rebecca Stadtlander to be identified as illustrator
of this work has been asserted in accordance with
the Copyright, Designs and Patents Act 1988

This book has been typeset in Times, Bellevue and Athelas

Printed in China

British Library Cataloguing in Publication Data:
a catalogue record for this book is available
from the British Library

ISBN 978-1-4063-9434-4

www.walker.co.uk

Also about Shakespeare:

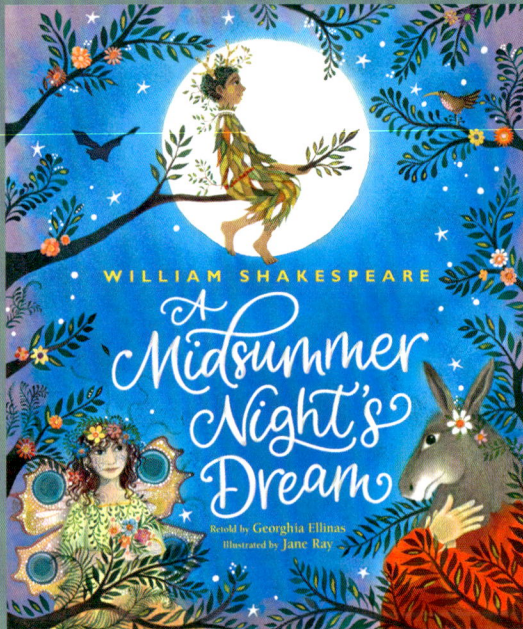

978-1-5295-1881-8

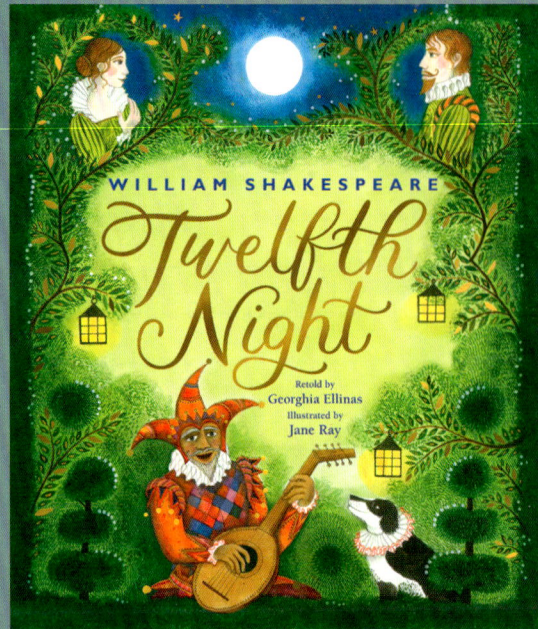

978-1-5295-0214-5

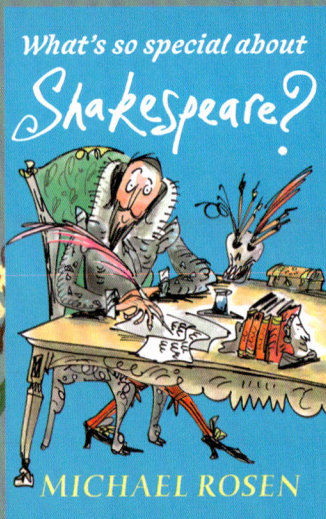

978-1-4063-6741-6

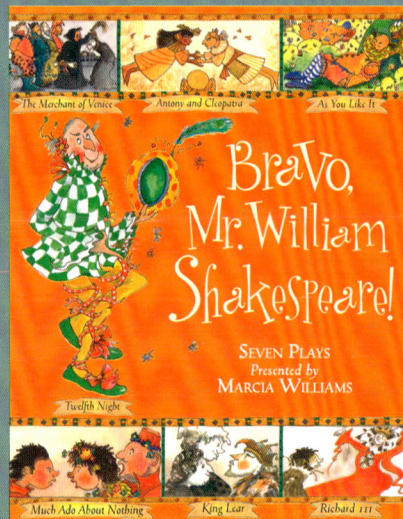

978-1-4063-2335-1

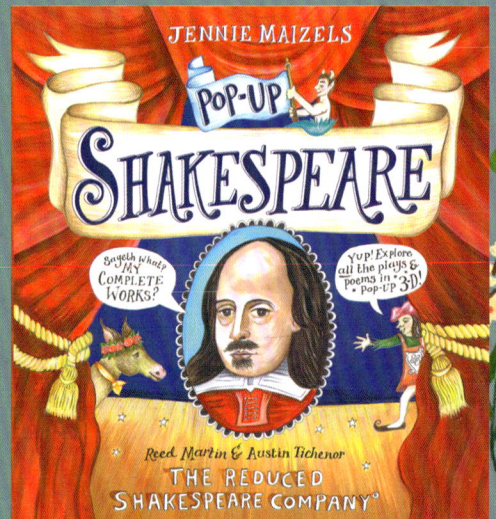

978-1-4063-7107-9

Available from all good booksellers

www.walker.co.uk